SEEDING YOUR SOUL

SEEDING YOUR SOUL

Six Considerations for Spiritual Growth

Trust •
Generosity •
Love •
Transformation •
Forgiveness •
Healing •

by
Dianne R. Costanzo

Bolchazy-Carducci Publishers, Inc.
Wauconda, IL USA

Editor
Laurie Haight Keenan

Photography
© Copyright 2004 by Marianne Saieg
unless otherwise noted

Cover Design   *Design and Layout*
Adam Phillip Velez   Jody Lynne Cull

Cover illustrations
Broomstone butterfly © Robert Pickett/CORBIS
Farmer Sowing Seeds by Larry Moore © Images.com/CORBIS

Gospel passages based on the King James Version

Greek quotations from *Novum Testamentum Graece,* 25th ed.
Edited by Eberhard Nestle and Kurt Aland.
(Stuttgart: Wuerttembergische Bibelanstalt, 1898 and 1927)

Bolchazy-Carducci books are available at special quantity discounts. For more information, please write to Promotions, Bolchazy-Carducci Publishing, 1000 Brown Street, Unit 101, Wauconda, IL   60084 USA

Printed in the United States of America
2005
by Worzalla

BOLCHAZY-CARDUCCI PUBLISHERS, INC.
1000 Brown Street, Unit 101
Wauconda, Illinois 60084 USA
www.bolchazy.com

ISBN: 0-86516-592-0

Library of Congress Cataloging-in-Publication Data
Costanzo, Dianne R.
  Seeding your soul : six considerations for spiritual growth / by Dianne R. Costanzo.
      p. cm.
  Includes bibliographical references and index.
  ISBN 0-86516-592-0 (hardbound : alk. paper)
  1. Spiritual life--Christianity. I. Title.

BV4501.3.C689 2005
248.4--dc22
                                              2004024981

Contents

FOREWORD

S eeding Your Soul is an awesome little book that will lead those who are willing into ever deeper and more splendid views of themselves from within. Ah, that problem of spiritual growth, that illusive phantom of the soul grappling with God, life, death, self, and eternity!

Dianne R. Costanzo offers a buffet of insights, using well known and well loved scriptures as springboards into self-exploration. Spiritual exercises, following each scripture, can't help but assist the soul into growing, almost against one's will, as it were. Precious examples for me are Dr. Costanzo's insights into living better, not longer. She similarly grabbed my soul with an invitation to be grateful for the weeds in our lives, for what they have to teach us.

In a very special way, Dr. Costanzo draws a distinction between being "cured" and being "healed." It is a striking insight to recognize a cat offering "healing" when one is perhaps awaiting a "cure." "I experienced a sense of being fine, just as I was, from the inside out," she discovers. All cures are temporary; healing is forever. She experienced a spiritual leap, "I had an internal belief that everything was ok, just as it was." A leap we all can make if we choose to receive the gift of healing when it is offered. Even if it is "only" from a cat being used by God for a special moment in our lives.

What are these insights worth in a world fraught with heartache, difficulties, illness, and fear? What are they worth in a world that is infatuated with beauty, health, wealth, prestige, popularity, and power? "Is there something in need of healing in your life?" the author asks. The answer is, "Of course." This book then gives us direction on how to attain that goal. What indeed are these insights worth? They are beyond value.

There, our own personal journey of spiritual growth can begin. But how to start? Let this book count the ways: A candle in a dark room. Flash paper to teach forgiveness. A garden, an illness, an invitation to ask yourself "if you are really better off for not bringing some beauty into your life?" or, "If you do not like where you are, can you ask yourself what would it take to move to the place where you would like to be?"

This book invites each of us on a spiritual journey to consider six areas of exploration: Trust, Generosity, Love, Transformation, Forgiveness, and Healing. It is all here for the taking, in a simple yet complex journey into truth and hope.

I see three great uses for this small but powerful book: One, as an instrument for individual spiritual growth and study. Two, as a guide for a spiritual growth group. Three, as a resource for pastors and clergy as they seek to help others experience the wonder of genuine lifelong spiritual growth and spiritual health. This one solitary pastor can only say, thank you, Dr. Costanzo.

THE REVEREND LISLE J. KAUFFMAN

ACKNOWLEDGEMENTS

Two of the most important kinds of persons to me are teachers and friends, and God has graced me with so many. As I continue my journey, it becomes increasingly clear that these people move from one circle to the other—teachers become friends; friends, teachers—and they all need to be thanked for the gifts they have so freely given to me.

I so deeply honor my teachers. While I cannot name all of them, I would be remiss if I did not name those who in their unique way have left their fingerprints on my soul. Sister Mary Martin de Porres, R.S.M., who gave me the gift of music; Dr. Margaret O'Connell, who taught me to "polish my prose"; Sister Helen Weinfurter, who taught me to read more deeply; the late Dr. Mary Lederer Roby, who led me to the world of spirit; Dr. Harry Puckett, who believed in my vision and in me.

I also must thank all of the staff at the Institute for Spiritual Leadership, particularly Lucy Abbott Tucker, my spiritual director. Being at ISL has been a gift without measure.

In particular, I also honor my Aikido sensei: Shihan Fumio Toyoda (1947–2001). Of all my teachers,

Toyoda Sensei had the longest and most direct influence on my self-development. He is always with me. Thank you, Andy Sato Sensei, for taking the responsibility that was left behind and for helping me continue to refine my Aikido.

And to my friends. I have such deep and abiding love. Mary Komparda, you give me companionship filled with laughter and joy. Marilyn (Unni) Fernandez, Regina (Bunky) Boarman—the three of us are united in a bond that transcends time and space. Laurie Haight Keenan, not only my editor, but such a dear and deep friend from way back when. Chris, Jo, Janet, Trudi, and Sue. My brother Michael, and Mary Anne (Pitha), Claudia (Snowball), and Marc, my cousins.

To my publishers, Lou and Marie Bolchazy, with deepest gratitude for their willingness to take a chance on this book.

Finally, to all my family, who are now my ancestors in eternity. I love you all and feel your presence every day.

NOTHING IS EVER LOST

photograph by Marianne Saieg

THE PATH IS WAITING FOR YOUR STEP

An Invitation to Spiritual Growth

How does your garden grow? That line, familiar and quaint, actually asks a significant question, one which Voltaire would answer by stating that we must "cultivate our gardens." But how does your garden grow? What is in it? What needs to be pruned away, nurtured, manured, tended to?

In other words, what does your spiritual landscape look like? All of us would wish to say that only beautiful flowers and stunning perennials grow with an insouciant abundance that would make us sigh. But then there are the weeds—and there are always weeds, those pesky reminders that life is not perfect or always pretty.

Some of those weeds are no more than the minor irritations of getting stuck behind a milk truck when we need to be somewhere fifteen minute ago. Some weeds are the annoying way other people eat. Some weeds, the more difficult to get to the root of, are our own flaws, idiosyncrasies, or mindsets that subvert us and prevent us from living life as our best selves.

One of the most delightful realizations that people often come to is that they really do have a choice in how they will cultivate their inner lives. In the beginning, some people are concerned that if they ask the question, they will be compelled to become Peace Corps workers or to turn away from a potentially lucrative career. So some resist asking the question for fear they might have to change. Most, however, come to understand that neither I nor the question itself is asking them anything at all, merely to consider the possibility that our lives are not just givens—we have the choice to respond how we will—and our choices create our interior landscape.

While I would love that all my students and spiritual directees choose to live a life of deep integrity, intelligence, and service, I am most struck by the voiced and silent fears surrounding their engagement with what appears on the surface a most benign question. Many of us know at a deep, mysterious level that the answer lies within. That is why many of us don't ask. We know that if we are really going to ask the question, the answer will invariably come, and we might not like what we hear. Asking leaves us wide open, creates a vulnerability, diminishes our illusionary control of life. In a time in our human history where technology has created the potential for so much good and misuse, we have become a culture of rapid-fire answers, quick fixes, and instant messaging. In and of themselves, such things are neither good nor bad. They are part of the terrain of twenty-first–century life. Not only is technology not going away, it will increasingly gain speed. No one who has ever emailed a friend in another country, benefited from medical advances, or found a cheap airfare on the internet would argue for eschewing such modern methods for improving our everyday lives.

Here's the good news. I am not asking anyone to stop the clock (which is now digitized and capable of calibrating micro-seconds). I am simply asking that we pause and cultivate the art of contemplation. Learning the art of waiting for things to be revealed cannot be mastered by scrutinizing life on the aforementioned clock. Very often, "getting" something more quickly is not necessarily better than getting it by and by.

Any gardener knows that cultivating a garden is a process, and as the years go by, the garden comes slowly and mysteriously into its own. Gardens often surprise their tenders because it is easy to forget what has been planted years before. Imagine the delight of seeing the Asian lilies emerging after a few years of non response.

And so this book, *Seeding Your Soul,* is a meditation, an invitation to spiritual growth, and I hope a companion on the journey of your own self-realization. I have a story to tell here that illustrates how impetus for such growth can come to us in small, at times surprising packages. I study Aikido, a Japanese martial art that emphasizes harmonizing with another's energy. Aikido (pronounced "Eye-KEY-Dough") actually means "the way of harmony through energy." Instead of trying to stop energy, Aikido blends with it, and by doing so can either employ joint locks or throws to neutralize someone else's attack. Aikido is very much a defensive practice whose aim is to control the situation without doing any harm. It is one way of putting body and mind together; it is the way that has worked for me, although there are many other ways—yoga, jogging, anything that makes you feel really connected to yourself. I have practiced Aikido for over sixteen years now, and it has been my privilege and honor to have studied directly under Shihan ("Master teacher") Fumio Toyoda for over thirteen of those years.

Anyone who had ever seen Toyoda Sensei (title of respect meaning "teacher") teach can attest to his incredible power and grace. He could move without moving and could feel like a tidal wave or be as gentle as a morning breeze. He taught with extraordinary clarity and humor. He knew who he was.

Sensei was teaching an afternoon class. I had been training for just a few months. About ten minutes before class ended, a drunk man stepped into the dojo, looked at Sensei, and shouted, "I'm going to kick your

___!" (You can fill in the blank.) Sensei responded in his thick Japanese accent, "You wanta kicka my ___? Ok, but you have to wait after class is over." Surprisingly, the man waited. After class, we all bowed, but no one left the mat. I thought to myself, "Oh my God. Sensei could pulverize this guy." Sensei bowed off the mat and walked to the door. He said, "Ok, you can kicka it now, but we go outside. After you."

The man went outside. Sensei held the door open for him, and after the man stepped out, Sensei locked the door, turned to us, and said, "He wanted to kicka my___," and laughed. Then we walked across the mat and went into his office. It was one of the most important lessons I learned from Sensei, and I learned many. He knew who he was and who this other man was, and he did beautiful Aikido in that moment. He blended his energy, led the man out, and maintained the man's dignity. In responding the way he did, Sensei showed through his example what his interior landscape was. His inner garden was filled with grace, humility, compassion, intelligence, and always humor.

On July 4, 2001, Toyoda Sensei died suddenly of a bacterial infection. That year, all my day lilies bordering the south side of my home were woefully delayed. Everyone else's lilies were open and full, but not mine. I received a phone call around 10:00 A.M.

that Sensei had died. Shocked and filled with grief, I walked around my home, sat in various chairs, called my friends. Then I went out the back door to sit in my garden. Out of habit, I looked to my left, and saw just one day lily fully in bloom. I was stunned by the mysteriously kind message the universe delivered.

At that moment something took root inside me and "ensouled" me, planting a seed of hope. So this book, aptly titled *Seeding Your Soul,* offers six meditations or "considerations"in which six different Gospel passages are presented as vehicles of tilling our interior soil. In order, we shall *consider* planting trust, generosity, love, transformation, forgiveness, and healing. While these particular virtues could be discussed in any order, it was my intention to look at how growing trust can lead to becoming more generous, and when we feel generous, we might feel open to love, and how our growing capacity to love transforms us to embrace forgiveness, and in our forgiveness we are healed. Each Gospel passage is offered and is viewed through the lens of different stories. After these considerations are cultivations, nurturing exercises and some tools that are meant to help us slow ourselves down and allow the Mystery we call God to tend to us as we tend to our interiority. Gracing the text are photographs by my friend and colleague, Marianne Saieg, OSF. Through the lens of her camera, Marianne invites us into contemplating how fragile and resilient the stuff of every day life actually is.

In the increasing speed and demands of life, our inner growth is something that we feel the need to attend to but very often put off. It is my hope that this little book will provide some way to brighten your day, offer some glance at the wonders of everyday life, and suggest that miracles happen when we least expect.

I invite you to consider.

DIANNE R. COSTANZO
Oak Park, Illinois
Summer, 2004

BE LIGHT FOR THE WORLD

CARRYING THE SEED OF GOD

This is the voice of Truth
This is the spark of the Universe, which is uniquely yours
This is your heart's deepest desire
This is the word God has spoken to you, only to you
It is what calls you to your best self
It is what remains when all else falls away from you
It is beyond your mind, for you are more than your mind
It is beyond your body, for you are more than your body
It is beyond your emotions, for you are more than your
  emotions
It is more than your achievements, more than your money,
    more than your belongings
It is more than your piety, more than your devotions,
    more than your prayers and your fasts and your beliefs
It is even more than your image of God. It is God.
It is the Godness inside you
        Naked, unadorned, unashamed
        Free, light, unencumbered
        Playful, open, buoyant
        Fluid, fiery, grounded, breathing

To touch it, you must get your hands dirty
To hold it, you must fall into the dark,
    perhaps for a very long time.
You will drown before you are blessed
You will burn before you are inspired
You will have to die many times, more than you can count
And through it all, what you desire has never left you,
never betrayed you, never sold you to strangers,
But has been with you, before time, waiting for your
  return.

DIANNE R. COSTANZO

WE ARE MORE THAN WE THINK WE ARE

Consider the Lilies
Luke 12:22–31

And Jesus said to his disciples, "Therefore I say to you, Do not be anxious for your life, what you shall eat; neither for the body, what you shall put on. Life is more than meat, and the body is more than raiment.

"Consider the ravens: for they neither sow nor reap; they neither have storehouse nor barn, and God feeds them: how much more are you better than the birds? And who of you with being anxious can add to his/her stature one bit? If you then are not able to do that thing which is least, why be anxious for the rest?

"Consider the lilies, how they grow: they toil not, they spin not; and yet I say to you, that Solomon in all his glory was not arrayed like one of these. If then God so clothe the grass, which is today in the field, and tomorrow is cast into the oven; how much more will he clothe you, O you of little faith?

"And seek not what you shall eat, or what you shall drink, neither be of doubtful mind. For all these things do the nations of the world seek after, and your Father knows that you have need of these things. But rather seek the kingdom of God, and all these things shall be added unto you."

photograph by Marianne Saieg

BELIEVE!

CONSIDER...PLANTING TRUST

οὐδὲ Σολομὼν ἐν πάσῃ τῇ δόξῃ αὐτοῦ
περιεβάλετο ὡς ἓν τούτων

...Solomon in all his glory
was not arrayed like one of these

"Trust me." How often do we say those
words; how often do we hear those words?
How often have we stepped out in faith
only to be betrayed, discounted, ignored? Trust is a
complex response to the mystery of life. The word
itself is simple—living it out is not.

In the age of information glut, sound bytes, "one,
two, three" formulae for a happy life, and enlight-
enment workshops, something as non-glamorous as
trust stares at us like a scar. It is a trace, a reminder of
a reality of something both evanescent and substan-
tial, something difficult to grasp yet undeniably solid.
It is foundational to any real and true development of
soulfulness. It is not something you can simply read
about and then "have" or "possess." It refuses to sit

on someone's tick list of things to do today. Like any spiritual discipline, it is simply a practice, one that requires your attention. It is often the onion in the soup. It has to be peeled and diced, and often it makes you cry before you can taste its sweetness.

And yet...we can certainly learn about trust by considering the lilies of the field. Neither toiling nor spinning, they just are themselves without added adornment or justification. If I am to read this Gospel passage and take it to heart, does it mean that I should not worry about paying the mortgage, feeding the kids, or setting something aside for retirement? Of course not. The Gospel does not suggest that we forsake our responsibilities. It merely suggests a mindfulness to help us carry those responsibilities out.

My father was a tailor. He had a little shop on the southwest side of Chicago and behind the store, he planted a garden. Originally, this snatch of land was a parking space made of asphalt. But he tilled it, turned the soil, made a fence, and cultivated his garden. Whatever he planted grew. At first, we saw this as a nice little hobby for Di (pronounced "Dee," his nickname). Sometimes, and more often than not, we saw it as an impediment to his doing his work because he would often leave the store unlocked and go into his garden. On warm spring and summer days, I would find him sitting on his haunches in the garden.

"What are you doing?" I would yell from the back door of the store. "I'm watching my eggplants grow," he would beam.

In addition to eggplants, my father grew the obligatory tomatoes, green peppers, basil, and green beans; not to mention roses, carnations, petunias, and grapes. To say that the garden grew is an understatement. It exploded with flowers and vegetables. One day my father picked twenty-two pounds of green beans. The next day eighteen pounds. The day after fourteen pounds. My mother cleaned and froze them, but after a point, she threatened him not to bring one more bean into the house! So my father would make bags to give his customers when they picked up cleaning and alterations. Some would get green beans (Thank God!), others tomatoes, others still grapes. One year yielded over four hundred pounds of grapes, so you can only imagine what my poor mother would have had to do with all that, had he not given a lot of it away.

Some people might say that my father had a green thumb. I believe he had a green heart. What some people saw as a hobby or a gift or even a diversion from work, I have come to understand as an extension of himself. He was a generous man, and I believe he was generous because he had an unshakable trust that God would provide. He was a most spiritually awake soul—not religious, as many Italian men are not. He went to church on Christmas and Easter. Yet his inborn goodness was something he lived out and celebrated every day of his life. His cathedral was nature. He was a keen observer of how life happens, and somehow, mysteriously, he learned the secret and because he learned it, everything around him grew.

I remember one night when I was about seven or eight. My mom, dad, brother and I were sitting on the back porch of our house eating fruit and enjoying a summer night. My father had just finished eating a peach. Holding the pit between his fingers, he thought out loud, "I wonder if there is a tree in here." Cavalierly, he tossed it into the backyard. The following spring, we saw something shooting up from the ground. A few years later the tree was bearing fruit.

Yes, my father was a gifted, although casual, gardener. Things grew for him, not so much, I think, because he was systematic and methodical—we know he wasn't—but because he believed things would grow. He trusted that anything, whether it was green beans or roses or people, would develop with faith. His optimism was not an antidote for sadness or suffering; it was not a quick fix. His belief in the goodness and sweetness in life did not deny life's ugliness and brutality, and his charisma and charm, his enthusiasm and appetite for living did not buffer him from dying from lung cancer. He had learned so deeply and so well that everything comes into the world and then someday must leave it. The former would not prevent the latter. In fact, it is because we are born that we die. But the secret my father taught me, so simple though not so easy, was to live in the moment. Enjoying the flowers growing doesn't make any of us live longer, just better.

photograph by Marianne Saieg

LIFE ALWAYS WINS

Exercises for Nurturing Trust

1. Go to the florist and buy some flowers. Put them in the prettiest vase you have and set them on a table. As the days go by, be attentive to how the flowers open, how they fill the room with fragrance. If you are worrying about some event in your life, sit down in front of your flowers and just watch them. Notice the ever so slight shifts in your own attitudes as the days pass. When the flowers have wilted and you have discarded them, repeat this exercise. If you are worrying that you do not have enough money for flowers, ask yourself if you are really any better off for not bringing some beauty into your life. You might think about ways in which you could afford them, like giving up smoking, forgoing needless trips to the vending machine for snacks that are expensive both in terms of money and calories. Be intentional to be attentive. My guess is that by looking at all the ways you throw money at needless and even harmful things, you would have enough money to buy flowers.

2. Cultivate a garden, even if you live in a small apartment. Plant flowers, herbs, vegetables—anything you like. As you tend to your garden, try talking to your plants. If you have a back yard, (a front yard will certainly do, too, if you are not shy), get down in the

grass and speak to it and the flowers that you have planted. Encourage them to grow and thank them for bringing so much beauty into your life. Now go one step further. Be grateful even for the weeds—they are part of nature's growth, too, and while you may not like them, they have something to offer. Figure out what the weeds represent for you and ask the figurative weeds in your life what they are trying to teach you.

Tools for Cultivating Trust

Books:

When Things Fall Apart: Heart Advice for Difficult Times by Pema Chödrön (Shambhala Press, 1997).

This book is a wonderful account by an American Buddhist nun of how she came to learn that things do indeed fall apart and how that can often be an opening to a different relationship with pain, disappointment, and grief.

Care of the Soul: A Guide for Cultivating Depth and Sacredness in Everyday Life by Thomas Moore (Harper Perennial, 1992).

Moore makes a powerful distinction between "curing" and "caring" for the soul. A psychotherapist, Moore relates his discovery that psychology is really about the soul, not the mind, and that most of us need to take care of our souls, whose primary work is the imagination.

MOVIES:

"Moonstruck" with Cher and Nicholas Cage.

Set in modern-day Brooklyn, this romantic comedy tells the tale of an Italian-American widow who initially becomes engaged to a man but who falls in love with his brother. Cher plays Loretta, the widow, who learns to trust God's plan for her, which is very different from her own plan.

"It's a Wonderful Life" with Jimmy Stewart and Donna Reed.

This Christmas favorite tells the story of a young man who wishes to leave Bedford Falls to see the world. Somehow, he never really leaves and slowly discovers, with the help of an adorable rookie angel named Clarence, that he is exactly where he needs to be.

OPEN UP TO LIFE

The Widow's Mite
Mark 12: 41–44

And Jesus sat over against the treasury, and saw how the people cast money into the treasury: and many that were rich cast in much.

And there came a certain poor widow, and she threw in two mites, which make a farthing.

And Jesus called his disciples to him, and said to them, "Verily I say to you, that this poor widow has cast more in, than all they who have cast into the treasury: for all they did cast in out of their abundance; but she out of her want did cast in all that she had, even all her living."

THE WORLD IS ALWAYS GIVING OF ITSELF

CONSIDER...PLANTING GENEROSITY

αὕτη δὲ ἐκ τῆς ὑστερήσεως αὐτῆς
πάντα ὅσα εἶχεν ἔβαλεν,
ὅλον τὸν βίον αὐτῆς

...but she out of her want
did cast in all that she had,
even all her living ...

Generosity is a funny thing: the more you give, the more you apparently have. But until you know how to give, it is difficult to believe you will always have enough. Many people who work in the field of spirituality have noted the choice we have between scarcity and abundance. If we move from the position of scarcity, then nothing we have will ever be enough. If, however, we move from the place of abundance, then we seemingly have more than enough.

I would like to draw a line between scarcity and abundance, creating a structure of tension between these two qualities of soulfulness. Scarcity, it seems, makes us smaller. When we feel threatened, under attack, defensive, we naturally close ourselves off from the world. People who operate from the position of scarcity are often frightened. They are the ones who are always counting their money, their time, their effort, measuring it out in a tit for tat exactitude, which can tire even the most robust soul. We are fatigued by these folks, and are often worn out for them because they spend so much of their energy making sure they are not cheated in any way. Ironically enough, they are cheated by their own fear of being cheated. In their effort to make sure that they get their due, that is exactly what they get and no more than that because nothing more could be allowed into themselves.

And then there is abundance. Abundance is full figured and big hearted. Somehow, people who live from the posture of abundance always seem to have more than enough. There is always room for one more chair around the kitchen table, even if someone has to sit on a crate. In the homes of those who live in abundance, there is always something to eat and drink. It might not be more than rice and beans or a dish of pasta, but everyone has something. Those who live from the place of abundance don't get permanently rattled when hardship comes. It is as if they know that the wheel of life always turns. If they are under the wheel and are living through difficulty, even heartache, somehow they know that the wheel turns eventually and they will one day be moving back toward the top. Conversely, when things are going splendidly, they can enjoy the moment and not get too attached to the comfort, for this, too, passes. These people have a balance—they know that things come and go, that life is bigger than they are, that the art of non-resistance allows them to participate in the moment fully and even joyfully, and as if by magic or mystery, they are always provided for.

The widow in Mark's Gospel exemplifies this quality. Jesus is in the temple noticing how people come in to worship. The wealthy put in large sums of money, not so much because they are generous, but because they want others to think that they are generous. They make quite a fanfare and are rewarded instantly by all the oohs and aahs of others. Then the widow comes in and quietly places her two coins in the collection box. No one but Jesus even sees her because, in the eyes of society, she is not important. She is a widow, so her place in society has been lost. She is poor, so she doesn't even have a place in society due to her economic status. This widow poses no threat to the wealthy men who are busy playing the game of one-upmanship of seeing and raising the ante at the collection box. While the wealthy in this Gospel seemingly make giving into an act about their importance, the widow simply gives of herself, and therein lies the difference. Real generosity is not about the amount, but about the heart of the person who gives.

And it is certainly not about romanticizing poverty and bashing those with money because we all know of wealthy people who are genuinely giving and grateful and poorer people who are just jealous that they don't have more money. It really is about sharing whatever you have—money, time, talent, kindness. We sadly live in a society that defines wealth exclusively by the size of one's bank account when in reality there are many very wealthy people whose income is less than impressive. There is a story about a young couple that gets married and the bridegroom says to his new bride, "I'm going to work very hard and someday we'll be rich." She looks at him with great love and responds, "We're already rich, maybe someday we'll also have money."

Ultimately, generosity concerns itself with sharing whatever one has. And I believe that a companion to generosity is humility. It seems that truly generous people are also humble. When the Magi presented baby Jesus with coffers of gold, frankincense, and myrrh, the little drummer boy, according to a favorite Christmas song, could offer only playing on his drum. That was enough. Next to the other gifts, playing a drum might appear meager and insufficient, but appearances are not always what they seem. Little things have their place among the larger things, and sometimes because of their diminutive size, they are worth as much or more proportionally. My mother always told me, "You can be generous with two cents and miserable with a million dollars." There is room for any and all giving if it comes from that humble place inside our hearts.

LIGHT GIVES MORE LIGHT

Exercises for Nurturing Generosity

1. Sit down in your favorite part of your home or garden. Light candles or incense, play soothing music. Close your eyes and imagine your soul as a wonderful palace, exquisitely furnished with love, compassion, generosity, forgiveness, patience, fortitude, wonder. Examine each quality fully—take them in your hands, feel their texture. Shake them gently. Do they make any sound? Are they wrapped up? What colors are they? How do you feel when you hold them?

Now think about the person(s) to whom you would like to give these gifts. Imagine the faces of the recipients of these gifts. Are they surprised, shocked, elated, dumbfounded? Imagine how you would feel to give such gifts.

As you contemplate this scene, do you notice any hesitation or fear or even anger inside yourself? Don't try to brush this away or ignore it. Rather, allow these feelings to be with you. Do they have anything to say to you?

2. Take a piece of paper and write the word "scarcity" on the left-hand side of the page. On the right-hand side across from it, write the word "abundance." Draw a line between these two words and imagine yourself as a tightrope walker traversing from one side to the

other. Note where you are on the line today. Is this place where you would like to be or would you like to move down the line? If you like where you are, then simply enjoy that place. If you do not like where you are, can you ask yourself what would it take to move to the place where you would like to be? Do you have what it takes to move? What is preventing you from taking even the smallest step toward that place?

TOOLS FOR CULTIVATING GENEROSITY

BOOKS:

Shambhala: The Sacred Path of the Warrior by Chogyam Trungpa (Shambhala Press, 1984).

This book offers a different insight into allowing ourselves to be persons of spiritual courage and compassion, which Trungpa suggests comes from entering the world of the broken heart. Such a journey creates a sense of generosity of soul.

Traveling Mercies: Some Thoughts on Faith by Anne Lamott (Pantheon, 1999).

In a wonderful and wacky way, Lamott shares the untidy path of her own spiritual growth, including failure and the grace to accept it as a learning.

MOVIES:

"Secondhand Lions" with Michael Caine and Robert Duvall.

Two crusty old brothers reluctantly raise a nephew who has been dropped off. In the process of dealing with this uninvited guest, they learn a new reason to live and in so doing teach the young boy how to be a man.

"Boys on the Side" with Whoopi Goldberg, Mary-Louise Parker, and Drew Barrymore.

Sharing a car going west, three women form a friendship that becomes a moving testament to the power of self-giving and the slow, non-negotiable power of love.

The Penitent Woman
Luke 7:36–50

And one of the Pharisees desired that Jesus would eat with him. And Jesus went into the Pharisee's house, and sat down to a meal.

And, behold, a woman in the city, who was a sinner, when she knew that Jesus sat at a meal in the Pharisee's house, brought an alabaster box of ointment, and stood at his feet behind him weeping, and began to wash his feet with tears, and wiped them with the hairs of her head, and kissed his feet, and anointed them with the ointment.

Now when the Pharisee who had invited Jesus saw this, he spoke to himself, saying, "This man, if he were a prophet, would have known who and what kind of woman this is that touches him: for she is a sinner."

And Jesus answering said to him, "Simon, I have something to say to you."

And he said, "Master, say on."

"There was a certain creditor who had two debtors: the one owed five hundred pence, and the other fifty. And when they had nothing to pay, he frankly forgave them both. Tell me therefore, which of them will love him most?"

Simon answered and said, "I suppose that he, to whom he forgave most."

And Jesus said to him, "You have rightly judged." And he turned to the woman, and said to Simon, "Do you see this woman? I entered into your house, you gave me no water for my feet: but she has washed my feet with tears, and wiped them with the hairs of her head. You gave me no kiss: but this woman since the time I came in has not ceased to kiss my feet. My head with oil you did not anoint: but this woman has anointed my feet with ointment. Wherefore I say to you, 'Her sins, which are many, are forgiven; for she loved much: but to whom little is forgiven, the same loves little.'"

And he said to the woman, "Your sins are forgiven."

And they that sat at the meal with him began to say within themselves, "Who is this that forgives sins also?"

And Jesus said to the woman, "Your faith has saved you, go in peace."

LOVE HOLDS MORE LOVE

CONSIDER...PLANTING LOVE

ᾧ δὲ ὀλίγον ἀφίεται,
ὀλίγον ἀγαπᾷ

...but to whom little is forgiven,
the same loves little

L ove really is an act of extension, making the one who loves move beyond him/herself, past shyness, convenience, even social approval. In this Gospel, a woman, who is known in town to be a "sinner," comes into the Pharisee's home and begins to wash the feet of Jesus with her tears. Obviously, the Pharisee and the other guests, all respectable men, create a stir. They do more than chastise Jesus for allowing the woman even to touch him; they set up a familiar "us versus them" dynamic often seen in many Gospel stories to drive home some significant points: (1) The people in places of esteem and privilege and power usually fail to get what Jesus means, and (2) These same people, by driving a wedge between themselves and the "sinners," those persons who do

not deserve to be in the same room with "their bet-
ters," these self-named worthies also fail to see how
close they actually are to those whom they hold in
contempt.

One of my favorite childhood memories was going to see Walt Disney's "Dumbo" with my mother. I
was struck by how cute that baby elephant with the
big ears was, and I watched horrified as people and
other prideful pachyderms shunned him when they
discovered his difference, his flaw, his sin. He became
the butt of jokes and other people's amusement, even
becoming a prop for the clowns' ridiculous firefight-
ing skit.

Fortunately, he is befriended by an unlikely companion, Timothy the mouse, and they go off and have
their adventures, including a poignant encounter
with a bunch of roughneck crows who teach Dumbo
to believe in himself. As I have continued to watch
"Dumbo" over the years, I am constantly struck by
the underlying sociological message in the film. Obviously, the main theme of overcoming a weakness
to make it into a strength is clear. A bit less clear,
however, might be that Dumbo could not have discovered his strength because of, not in spite of, his
difference without the help of those fortunate others who miraculously enter his life just as he needs
them to do so. Who would think that a mouse, of all

critters, would come to the aid of an elephant? Who could imagine that a bunch of cigar-smoking, jive-talking crows, usually perceived as carrion feeders and pests in general, would be the ones to build the little elephant's self-esteem?

Yet love does the seemingly impossible, allowing us to give and receive in ways we might have thought unimaginable. Love in this Gospel story (and also in "Dumbo") seems to be juxtaposed to pride. It's the classic match up between the "haves" and the "have-nots," between the "ins" and the "outs." Oddly enough, those who "have" and are "in" have much more to lose than those who "have not" and are "out." The woman in this Gospel does not care about the ridicule of the Pharisees. For all we know, they might be some of her best customers. Her attention is completely and solely on Jesus. She treats him with a hospitality and reverence that the host cannot even begin to fathom. Simon, the host, provided no water for Jesus to wash his feet with, yet she washed his feet with her tears. Simon did not greet Jesus with a kiss, but she unceasingly kissed his feet. This woman, whose name we never know, is the counterpoint to Simon.

To push this farther, it seems that Simon meets Jesus eye to eye; the woman sees Jesus with the eyes of the heart, which allows her to wash his feet. It is not an act of humiliation, of servitude, but an act of humility and of love. Within the context of the Gospels, we will see this enacted again during the Last Supper when Jesus washes the feet of his disciples and gives the mandatum to serve others. It is a radical act, a reversal of ego, a turning over of the social order. And as unbelievable as it may appear, it is precisely what allows sweet baby elephants to fly. It's the miracle we all have inside ourselves if we are blessed with friends who come into our lives and walk with us as we discover our inherent gifts, which are often hidden in our deepest flaws.

LOVE FLINGS ITSELF INTO CREATION

photograph by Marianne Saieg

COME TO KNOW YOURSELF IN A DEEPER WAY

Exercises for Nurturing Love

1. In a quiet place, set two chairs: one for you and one for the thing that you find your biggest weakness. This could be something strictly physical (your weight, a facial characteristic, a body part that you don't like, a scar from surgery) or non-physical (a speech impediment, a limp, a learning disability). Have a conversation with this weakness. Ask it anything you would like; for instance, "Hey, speech impediment, do you know how much you embarrassed me as a child?" Now, sit in the chair reserved for your weakness and take on the role of that weakness. Have it speak back to you. It may say something like, "I know I was hard for you to live with, but without your knowing it, I also gave you a perspective that you would not have had." Continue this dialogue and see what comes of it. You may discover that your weakness also had something of value.

2. In a journaling exercise, write your own obituary. What would you want people to know about you? List all your accomplishments, your degrees, promotions, etc. In reality, without diminishing your achievements, how important are they to you? Now, write down those things you never said or did because you felt trapped by social convention or approbation. Go

through both lists and focus on one thing that most strikes you.

On another sheet of paper, draw a line down the middle. On one side of the line, write your name at the top, on the other side, the name of the thing that most strikes you. Have a dialogue with that accomplishment or unsatisfied desire. What does it have to tell you?

TOOLS FOR CULTIVATING LOVE

BOOKS:

The Collected Works of St. John of the Cross translated by Kieran Kavanaugh, OCD, and Otilio Rodriguez, OCD (ICS Publications, 1973).

One of the most beloved classics of spirituality, the poetry of St. John of the Cross passionately communicates how the soul longs for union with God.

The Soul of Rumi: A New Collection of Ecstatic Poems translated by Coleman Barks (Harper, 2001).

The poetry of this thirteenth-century Sufi mystic shatters the confines of life measured out in safe and predictable doses. At the heart of his work is what the mythologist Joseph Campbell calls "the radiance."

MOVIES:

"Edward Scissorhands" with Johnny Depp
and Winona Ryder.

Tim Burton's unconventional tale of love and self-discovery at first may seem like an offbeat fairy tale, but at its depth, the movie poignantly asks "what does it take to become a human being?" Edward must learn slowly how to fit into the sameness of suburbia, but his most radical lesson comes when he falls in love.

"The Color Purple" with Whoopi Goldberg and
Margaret Avery.

Celie, an abused young girl, is given in marriage to a man she calls Mr._____. For years, she merely exists, waiting for this life to be over until she learns through the love and friendship of Shug and Sofia that she has the right to "enter into the Creation."

photograph by Marianne Saieg

THERE IS NO PLACE WHERE GOD IS NOT

THE TRANSFIGURATION OF JESUS
Mark 9:2–8

And after six days Jesus took with him Peter, and James, and John, and led them up into a high mountain apart by themselves: and he was transfigured before them. And his raiment became shining, exceeding white as snow; so as no fuller on earth can white them.

And there appeared to them Elias with Moses: and they were talking with Jesus. And Peter answered and said to Jesus, "Master, it is good for us to be here: and let us make three tabernacles; one for you, and one for Moses, and one for Elias." For he knew not what to say; for they were sore afraid.

And there was a cloud that overshadowed them: and a voice came out of the cloud, saying, "This is my beloved Son: hear him."

And suddenly, when they had looked round about, they saw no man any more, save Jesus only with themselves.

THE WHEEL TURNS

photograph by Marianne Saieg

CONSIDER...PLANTING TRANSFORMATION

καὶ μετεμορφώθη ἔμπροσθεν αὐτῶν

...and he was transfigured before them.

There are certain moments in our lives when our true nature is revealed, not only to ourselves, but to those around us. It is as if the veil surrounding our true self is lifted, if only briefly, and the truth of ourselves is told to ourselves. Once we cross these thresholds, we cannot uncross them. We might lie about the truth, run away from it, deny it, betray it, but the truth always has its way and ultimately calls us to confess to it. We can bend the truth, but the truth, in its own time, bends back, calling us to accountability.

My father loved adages. I remember sitting at the dining room table with him night after night, he at the head of the table reading the *Chicago Sun-Times* or the *Chicago Tribune*, I to his right reading a book for school. There we were, silently reading together, when all of a sudden, out of the blue, he would proclaim, "Petunia (one of his many nicknames for me), the wheel of justice grinds slowly but grinds exceedingly well!" Then he would return to the paper. I wouldn't know what prompted him to break the quiet of the evening, but I came to expect spontaneous exclamations whenever we sat at the table.

Of course, it was entertaining, but as life continued to unfold for me, his utterances became great friends that have helped me in some of my darkest moments, sometimes providing solace, sometimes pointing the way for me to go. As I have grown, I cannot tell you how many times I have repeated that "the wheel of justice grinds slowly, but grinds exceedingly well" to myself, to friends, to students. That simple and strange axiom has become for me a touchstone, a reminder to tell the truth of myself to myself and let the truth have its way.

Truth and transformation go hand in hand. It is virtually impossible to break through to a deeper, more vivid understanding of life unless we live on and in the truth. To be at that place, however, is not always easy, convenient, or a guarantee of reward. Often, the opposite can be assured. D. H. Lawrence observes, "Are you willing to be sponged out, erased, cancelled, made nothing; / Are you willing to be made nothing?

/ Dipped into oblivion? If not, you will never, ever really change."

T. S. Eliot notes, "It is a condition of complete simplicity / Costing not less than everything."

The life of Jesus testifies to this. He was completely true to his nature, and his nature was revealed to those around him. In some ways, it would have been easy and ego affirming for Jesus to remain on the mountain. His close companions, Peter, James, and John, could have just pitched the tents and basked in the glory of witnessing such a vision. But Jesus does not choose to stay on the mountain; he comes down and continues his life, his teaching, his preaching, his miracles, and his inexorable journey to Jerusalem, to the cross, to his death, and ultimately to his resurrection. And he teaches us to do the same in our lives.

Interestingly enough, the passage in Mark's Gospel that precedes the Transfiguration account provides the doctrine of the cross: "Whoever would preserve his or her life will lose it, but whoever loses his or her life for my sake and the Gospel's will preserve it (Mark 8:35).

It is a law of the spirit, which pushes us toward a sense of mission and meaning. What good is our understanding, our work, our struggle if we do not give our gifts, however meager they seem to be to us, to the world. Our gifts, our attempts may be

misunderstood, even twisted to serve someone
else's schemes, but it is our coming to the truth of
ourselves and our willingness to give it to others that
transforms and transfigures us. Our willingness to
give ourselves away, to detach from the limits that we
put on ourselves makes us fuller and holy.

This is done in hundreds of different ways every
day in the commonality of our daily lives. Women
who give birth to children, men who become soldiers,
women and men who fight fires, fight crime, teach
children, save lives go beyond themselves all the time.
Those people who volunteer for causes important to
them, raise money to combat diseases, work in shel-
ters, donate money, pray for others' intentions all do
things that are bigger than themselves.

Transfiguration in our own lives often happens
in small, almost imperceptible ways—but, oh, the
difference it makes.

A CLEAN HEART BURNS WITH THE FIRE OF GOD

COME TO THE EDGE

EXERCISES FOR NURTURING TRANSFORMATION

1. Think about what calls you to your best self—perhaps it is raising your children or doing the work you are called to do. How much time do you actually spend doing these things? What has gotten in the way for you? What might you need to change to put your life in balance?

2. Reflect on a transformational moment in your life. How did it change you? What did it cost you? Now reflect on what you tell yourself about it. Tell the truth, now, and see for yourself whether you have broken through to a place of telling the truth without blame or judgment, or whether you have become stuck in the pain of the event and have used that to stop your life.

Tools for Cultivating Transformation

Books:

The Diving Bell and the Butterfly: A Memoir of Life in Death by Jean-Dominique Bauby (Alfred A. Knopf, 1997).

This remarkable book is the memoir of Bauby, an editor, who suffers a massive stroke, paralyzing him from head to toe. He wrote this book after being imprisoned in his body, literally by blinking his left eye (the only part of his body that functioned) at the alphabet strategically arranged on a piece of paper.

The Scarlet Letter by Nathaniel Hawthorne (many editions available).

Hester Prynne, accused of adultery, is humiliated in front of puritan Salem. While the townspeople can force her to wear the letter "A," they cannot really break her spirit, and she finds a way to become better, not bitter, and in so doing, the town slowly comes to admire her.

MOVIES:

"Frida" with Salma Hayek and Alfred Molina.

One of the most important figures in twentieth-century art, Frida Kahlo survives both illness and accident to emerge as a visionary artist who uses her life as the canvas upon which to paint her life. Not always pretty, her paintings, however, stare truth directly in the eye.

"Groundhog Day" with Bill Murray and Andie McDowell.

Sometimes we are doomed to repeat a lesson until we get it. Bill Murray plays a weatherman who keeps waking up to the same day until he wakes up inside himself.

THE PRODIGAL SON
Luke 15:11–31

And Jesus said, "A certain man had two sons: and the younger of them said to his father, 'Father, give me the portion of goods that fall to me.' And he divided between them his living.

"And not many days after the younger son gathered all together, and took his journey into a far country, and there wasted his substance with riotous living. And when he had spent all, there arose a mighty famine in that land; and he began to be in want. And he went and joined himself to a citizen of that country; and he sent him into his fields to feed swine. And he would gladly have filled his belly with the husks that the swine did eat: and no man gave any to him.

"And when he came to himself, he said, 'How many hired servants of my father's have bread enough and to spare, and I perish with hunger! I will arise and go to my father, and will say to him, "Father, I have sinned against heaven, and before you, and am no more worthy to be called your son: make me one of your hired servants."'

"And he arose, and came to his father. But when he was yet a great way off, his father saw him, and had compassion, and ran, and fell on his neck, and kissed him.

"And the son said to him, 'Father, I have sinned against heaven, and in your sight, and am no more worthy to be called your son.'

"But the father said to his servants, 'Bring forth the best robe, and put it on him; and put a ring on his hand, and shoes on his feet: and bring the fatted calf, and kill it; and let us eat, and be merry: for this my son was dead, and is alive again; he was lost, and is found.' And they began to be merry.

"Now his elder son was in the field: and as he came and drew close to the house, he heard music and dancing. And he called one of the servants, and asked what these things meant.

"And the servant said to him, 'Your brother has come; and your father has killed the fatted calf, because he has received him safe and sound.'

"And the elder son was angry, and would not go in: therefore his father came out, and entreated him.

"And he answering said to his father, 'Lo, these many years do I serve you, and I never at any time transgressed your commandment: and yet you never gave me a kid, that I might make merry with my friends: but as soon as this son came, who has devoured your living with harlots, you have killed for him the fatted calf.'

"And the father said to him, 'Son, you are ever with me, and all that I have is yours.'"

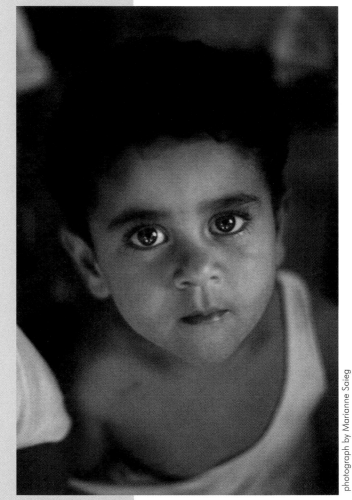

photograph by Marianne Saieg

YOU ARE ALWAYS MINE

Consider...Planting Forgiveness

σὺ πάντοτε μετ᾽ ἐμοῦ εἶ,
καὶ πάντα τὰ ἐμὰ σά ἐστιν

... you are ever with me,
and all that I have is yours.

"Waste not, want not," the old saying goes. "Youth is wasted on the
young." "That was a waste of time."
"Don't get wasted." We are constantly reminding ourselves not to squander our resources, our time, or our
money because to do so exposes our frailty and our
foolishness to others.

The Gospel of the Prodigal Son, a perennial
favorite among preachers, often is seen as a story
that warns of the wasteful ways of the younger child
and how a loving parent can forgive the young man's
imprudence, often at the amazement and disapproval
of the older and more temperate son. We all know
that the younger son asks for his share and strikes
out on his own. Not surprisingly, the money doesn't

last long and the boy is left without friends and resources. Odd how his good-time companions abandon him at the exact moment that his money runs out. He has to do something to live, so he takes on a job as a common laborer feeding pigs. "Coming to his senses at last" (15:17), the young man decides to go home and beg that he be treated as one of his father's hired hands.

We know the rest of the story. Seeing his son returning home, the father runs out to greet him and restore the boy to his rightful place in the family without wanting or needing to hear his son's act of contrition. Upon hearing that his brother has returned and that the father has called for a feast to celebrate, the older brother expresses his anger and resentment. How is it fair that the "sinner," the irresponsible baby, gets the fatted calf while the dutiful son doesn't even get a kid goat?

If truth be told, all of us have been the dutiful son. We have seen others who are undeserving of favor receive inheritances, get promotions, enjoy affection—and all our finger-pointing and recitation of others' failures and flaws won't change a thing.

If truth be told, all of us have also been the goof-off, the "golden child" who can do no wrong. And we have all been the parent who sees past the pain and the hurt to take someone back, even when others warn us not to be foolish.

In some way, each of the three characters is prodigal because each "wastes" something. The younger son wastes money and "blows it" on liquor and women. But he comes back to himself and does something proactive. Despite his lack of good judgment initially, he has the wherewithal to take a risk. He asks for his share, but notice, he does not ask for his brother's share nor does he leave his father in debt. He took what was his anyway. Yes, he loses it, but when he realizes his lesson, he has the humility to return home. He risks again because he does not presume his father will even acknowledge him. He returns without any expectation of being received and would have been thrilled to be treated as a worker. His prodigality is youthful indiscretion.

The father is prodigal, too, but in a much different way. His prodigal nature is his excessive generosity. When asked, he gives his son his share. Perhaps he is partly to blame for his son's failure because he might never have trained his children to be responsible. Whatever. When the young man returns, the father is prodigal again, this time in bestowing upon him unconditional love and forgiveness. Is he silly to do so? Perhaps, but sometimes such foolishness is God's wisdom. Love is ultimately and always foolish because it shatters the confining and punishing constrictions of the bean-counting, *i*-dotting and *t*-crossing measurements of a heart that is small.

And for that reason, it is the elder son who is most unexpectedly the most prodigal of all. Never asking for anything, he nevertheless expects everything and consequently wastes his life by storing up resentment and silently keeping count of his father's affection and money. He never risks taking his share and doing anything with it, good or bad. In the long run, it might be true that he never wasted his share of the inheritance; he does something much more harmful—he wastes the opportunity to love. When he complains that he has "slaved" for the father, never disobeying "an order," the father asks, "Don't you know that everything I have is yours?" Clearly, the elder son does not know his place and instead has wasted illimitable opportunities because he was too afraid or too arrogant to ask for anything. There is absolutely nothing in this Gospel to suggest that the father wound have denied the elder son anything or would have treated him differently had the tables been reversed and he had squandered his share.

When all is said and done, it is not so much as whether we are prodigal as it is how we are prodigal. We can waste our lives by not knowing how to manage what we ask for or we can waste our lives by sitting on the sidelines refusing to take a chance. Fortunately, forgiveness sees through and past our excesses and deficiencies, reminding us that we have a proper place, a home. All we have to do is ask.

photograph by Marianne Saieg

FORGIVENESS ALWAYS MAKES WAVES

Exercises for Nurturing Forgiveness

1. Whom or what do you need to forgive—a family member, coworker, friend? Is there something inside yourself that you can't let go of, something that has a hold on you? Ask yourself what this holding onto is doing to you. Is it making you bitter, small, petty? Is that how you wish to live out your days? Usually, our holding onto hurt occurs because we feel justified. While we may indeed be right about our being hurt, that does not necessarily make it right for us to poison ourselves. Ask yourself in the very depth of your being, "Can I make some room inside myself for forgiveness?" Forgiveness does not mean that you forget the hurt and it certainly does not mean that the person or event responsible for the hurt is not accountable. Forgiveness simply means that we can open a space inside ourselves for the possibility of healing. Whether things are fully resolved depends on the ability of all those concerned to meet without bitterness or vengeance.

2. Create a ritual or letting something that is binding you go. Ask yourself whether you are better off with or without the resentment. If you answer "Yes, but...," remember that the truth often comes after the "but." If you answer "Yes, but...," then you still might be

needing to hold onto the anger or resentment. Perhaps it gives you a sense of being right. Go back inside yourself and in that deepest part of yourself that is holy and true, can you make some room for peace? It doesn't have to be a great, big space—it doesn't have to eradicate all the hurt—just make *some* space. Light a candle or incense and bless that space inside you and ask that it grow.

3. Another kind of ritual is to go to a magic store and buy some flash paper. Sit in front of a beautiful lit candle and calm yourself. Write the name of the person or the name of the feeling inside you that you would like to forgive. Do not do this lightly, but only when you are truly ready to make some space inside yourself for forgiveness. Touch the paper to the fire and let it go; the paper will disappear. Know that by doing this you do not make all the hard feelings go away—you merely create some space for you to continue to let goodness grow inside of you.

TOOLS FOR CULTIVATING FORGIVENESS

BOOKS:
Peace is Every Step: The Path to Mindfulness in Everyday Life by Thich Nhat Hanh (Bantam, 1991).

Sometimes forgiveness can be touched by becoming more mindful that some hurt or wrong needs attending to. Such awareness doesn't "fix" anything; rather, it can allow us to be more present to the now, and very slowly, we can learn to free ourselves of the pain.

39 Ways to Open Your Heart: An Illuminated Meditation by Arlene Gay Levine, illustrated by Karen Kroll (Conari Press, 1996).

This illuminated meditation is so simple and lovely. With very few words, it arrests the heart's imagination to listen to one's inner truth.

MOVIES:

"Tribute" with Jack Lemmon and Robby Benson.

The story of father-son strife, it is a powerful reminder that our desire to be understood is always mixed with our fear to reveal ourselves to those who are most important to us.

"A League of Their Own" with Geena Davis and Lorri Petty.

As much as this is a wonderful movie about the women's league of baseball, it is also a story of two sisters (one who pitches, the other who catches) and their struggle to let the other be herself.

LET HEALING POUR INTO YOU

THE TEN LEPERS
Luke 17:11–19

And it came to pass, as Jesus went to Jerusalem, that he passed through the midst of Samaria and Galilee. And as he entered into a certain village, there met him ten men who were lepers, who stood afar off: and they lifted up their voices, and said, "Jesus, Master, have mercy on us."

And when he saw them, he said to them, "Go show yourselves to the priests." And it came to pass, that, as they went, they were cleansed.

And one of them, when he saw that he was healed, turned back, and with a loud voice glorified God, and fell down on his face at Jesus' feet, giving him thanks: and he was a Samaritan.

And Jesus answering said, "Were there not ten cleansed? But where are the nine? There are not found those who returned to give glory to God, save this stranger."

And Jesus said to him, "Arise, go your way: your faith has made you whole."

"Mimi" photograph by Mary Komparda

ALLOW YOURSELF TO BE SURPRISED

CONSIDER...PLANTING HEALING

ἡ πίστις σου σέσωκέν σε

...your faith has made you whole

On a beautiful Thursday morning in October of 1999, I started my day just like any other morning by going into the bathroom to brush my teeth. When I looked in the mirror, I realized that the left side of my face was completely paralyzed. The left side was erringly devoid of movement—my laugh lines gone, the corner of my mouth frozen, my eye snapped open. The right side was its usual mobile self and the juxtaposition of life and no life stunned me. At first, I wondered whether I was having a stroke, but I felt my left arm and I had no pain or discomfort at all. Then I realized I probably had Bell's Palsy, something I had heard of but knew next to nothing about. I must say that my capacity for denial could be extraordinary, so I figured that I would continue with my day and see how I was later. I went to school and taught my morning class at the university but returned home afterward fatigued. My face remained animated on one side, mockingly still on the other. Finally, I called my doctor and made an appointment.

Indeed, I had Bell's Palsy, which I learned is a virus that comes and goes pretty much by itself, and while I was given a five-day prescription of steroids, there was little else I could do but wait. I had to put drops into my left eye and patch it at night to protect it from drying out. I was told that this condition could last weeks or months or more. That was that.

The night after the diagnosis, I finally went to bed. I nestled in under the covers and began a simple prayer: "Dear God, let me feel your healing touch." I closed my one good eye and immediately felt something amazing. Mimi, my little black and white cat, who was just over a year old, jumped onto the bed, walked up my body, sat on my chest, and put her paw on the left side of my face and began purring. Such an immediate answer to my little prayer sent shivers throughout my body and I was filled with a tremendous sense of peace and calm. In the morning I awoke to find Mimi sitting on the chest of drawers, looking down at me. From that moment, I knew that Mimi was much more than a loving pet; she was my guardian angel, a furry reminder of God's unfailing love.

As it turned out, I was lucky. My face returned to normal in about three weeks. I was cured. But I believe I was also healed, and that occurred when Mimi, my silly and sweet cat, touched my face and purred, because in that moment, I felt something more than restoration of body. I experienced a sense of being fine, just as I was, from the inside out. While I was hoping for the external manifestation of good health, I had an internal belief that everything was ok, just as it was.

I went back to school to teach, obviously marred by the palsy. My students were very kind and supportive when I told them what had happened and that I did not know when the palsy would run its course. In the meantime, this was the way things were and I was ok. Life went on.

Am I glad that the case was mild and that my face regained mobility and texture? Yes, of course. Would I want to go through this again? No. Yet I can say that in that time, I felt good from the inside out. I was ok in not knowing when/if the palsy would leave, not because I don't care about my looks (I have a pronounced streak of vanity running through me, for sure), but because something deeper and truer and finer emerged for me. I felt God's presence in the thick of it, quietly assuring me that everything is all right, even when it is not all right. And in all of it, I could feel happy to be alive.

Perhaps that is what the one leper who returned to Jesus felt and he had to come back to Jesus to say thanks. Perhaps there is a profound difference between being cured and being healed, and while it is always wonderful for both to occur simultaneously, we need to be mindful that they are different enough. From the Gospel story we can see that all ten were made whole—all were cured. But only the one who could see past the exteriority to notice the inner truth of God's loving presence was also healed. That one leper somehow felt compelled to come back to the source, and maybe it is that need to return, that impulse to acknowledge the existent and persistent relationship between God and us that allows us to see ourselves as we really are, and in so doing, we are free to be whole.

photograph by Marianne Saieg

TURN TOWARD THE LIGHT

LORD, OPEN OUR EYES

Exercises for Nurturing Healing

1. Is there something in need of healing in your life? Can you name it? It may be a physical illness or an emotional wound. Quite possibly, your condition may not "get better" in the conventional sense. That does not mean, however, that you cannot experience healing, that feeling inside that transcends the outer condition. Imagine a place inside yourself that is free of disturbance, free of outer distractions, free of worry. Come to that inner place slowly; perhaps you can imagine descending a staircase. With each step down to your inner peace, commit to opening your heart just a little bit. By the time you get to the bottom of the stairs, it is not necessary that you have opened your heart completely—just enough for you to take in some healing presence. As you sit in this inner place of peace, *don't do anything!* Just sit and let it be. See what happens.

2. Find a quiet place in your home or garden. Sit in a comfortable position with your back straight and your hands in your lap, palms up. In one hand, imagine all the things that worry or distract you; in the other hand, imagine that you are holding a ball of healing energy. The ball, infinitely light and light giving, is a source of unlimited power. As you are aware of all the

burdens you hold in one hand, also be aware of the incredible lightness of healing energy in your other hand. If you can, allow the healing energy to send its warmth and light to aid what you hold in your other hand. Keep both hands open and simply become more aware of the exchange of being in both hands. You do not have to change anything, do anything, fix anything. Simply allow yourself the experience.

3. This exercise must be done at night. Go into your favorite room in your home with one candle and some matches, and draw the drapes, turn off the lights, and make the room as dark as possible. Sit in the darkness for a few minutes, with the unlit candle in front of you, allowing the darkness to envelop you. You may begin to get uncomfortable, wanting to turn on the lights or TV or to provide yourself with some distraction. Keep sitting in the darkness, and as you sit, bring up your concerns and troubles—don't shoo them away. Welcome them and let them be with you. The natural tendency is to try to analyze your problems and "what if" yourself to silliness. Please avoid this. Once again, don't do anything except be aware of what has come to visit you. Once you are fully aware of what has come to visit you, light the candle. Now continue to sit in what is not as dark. Instead of focusing on how

the room is not fully illumined, call your attention to how the room is not nearly as dark.

TOOLS FOR CULTIVATING HEALING

BOOKS:
Tuesdays with Morrie by Mitch Albom (Doubleday, 1997).

This beloved favorite will surely become a classic. Albom honors his teacher, Morrie, who is suffering from ALS. Even as Morrie's physical health deteriorates, he still shows his errant student that, to quote Auden, Morrie's favorite poet, "We must love each other or die."

King Lear by William Shakespeare (many editions available)

Perhaps the greatest of Shakespeare's dramas, this play tells the tale of a king who initially is more interested in being praised than he is of being the king and father he should be. Lear banishes his youngest daughter Cordelia for not lying to him. The reunion between father and daughter is the most heart-wrenching and healing in all of literature.

MOVIES:

"The Divine Secrets of the Ya-Ya Sisterhood" with Ashley Judd and Ellen Burstyn.

Vivi Walker is a force to be reckoned with. Her faithful friends love her, confront her, and are agents in her being healed once everyone decides to tell the truth. This enables Vivi finally to enter a full relationship with her daughter.

"What's Love Got to Do with It" with Angela Bassett and Laurence Fishburne.

Tina Turner is one of the great rock and roll divas of all time. This true story shows her struggle to free herself from an abusive marriage and start from scratch.

Other Sources for Contemplation and Growth

Bly, Robert. *The Soul Is Here for Its Own Joy.*
Hopewell, New Jersey: Ecco Press, 1995.

Brussat, Frederic and Mary Ann. *Spiritual Literacy:*
Reading the Sacred in Everyday Life. New York:
Scribner, 1996.

Campbell, Joseph. *Thou Art That.* Novato,
California: New World Library, 2001.

Carlson, Richard, and Benjamin Shield, eds.
Handbook for the Soul. Canada: Little, Brown &
Company, 1995.

Chödrön, Pema. *The Places That Scare You: A Guide to*
Fearlessness in Difficult Times. Boston: Shambhala,
2001.

Eliot, T. S. *The Complete Poetry and Plays.* New York:
Harcourt, Brace & World, Inc., 1971.

Oliver, Mary. *New and Selected Poems.* Boston:
Beacon Press, 1992.

Simmons, Philip. *Learning to Fall: The Blessings of an Imperfect Life.* New York: Bantam, 2000.

Wilber, Ken. *The Marriage of Sense and Soul: Integrating Science and Religion.* New York: Random House, 1998.

Zohar, Danah, and Dr. Ian Marshall. *SQ: Connecting with Your Spiritual Intelligence.* New York and London: Bloomsbury Publishing, 2000.

CONSIDERATIONS

CONSIDERATIONS

About the Author

Dianne R. Costanzo is a teacher, poet, and spiritual director. For over twenty-five years, she has taught literature, writing, and spirituality at the college level and to adults. She holds a Ph.D. in literature and a Masters in Pastoral Studies from Loyola University, Chicago. In addition, she studied at the Institute for Spiritual Leadership in Chicago.

A believer in the synergy of body, mind, and spirit, she is a student and certified teacher of Aikido, a Japanese martial art, and holds the rank of yondan (fourth-degree black belt) and the title Sensei; she is also a senior instructor of IMPACT Chicago, Self-Defense.

Currently, she is an adjunct professor at Dominican University and is on staff at the Institute for Spiritual Leadership. Dianne also has a private practice in spiritual direction and leads retreats, days and evenings of reflection, and workshops. In the fall of 2004, Dianne opened an Aikido dojo, One Point Center, in Oak Park, Illinois.

Dianne R. Costanzo may be contacted by email at: d.costanzo@juno.com.

About the Photographer

Marianne Saieg is a Joliet Franciscan, spiritual director, retreat facilitator, teacher, and photographer. Marianne's academic background/experience includes a Masters in Religious education from the University of St. Thomas, Houston, Texas; studies in Media Communication, Northern Illinois University; a Certificate in the Art of Spiritual Direction from Mercy Center in Burlingame, California; and a Masters in Pastoral Studies/Spirituality from Loyola University, Chicago. Marianne creates slide meditations, greeting cards, and photographic enlargements. It is "Through a Lens" that she believes a photograph exclusively captures, on film, a single moment, an image in time, a memory that lasts a lifetime.

Marianne Saieg may be contacted by mail at: Box 712, Westmont, IL 60559.